GRADE 2 WRITING

Fun-filled Activities

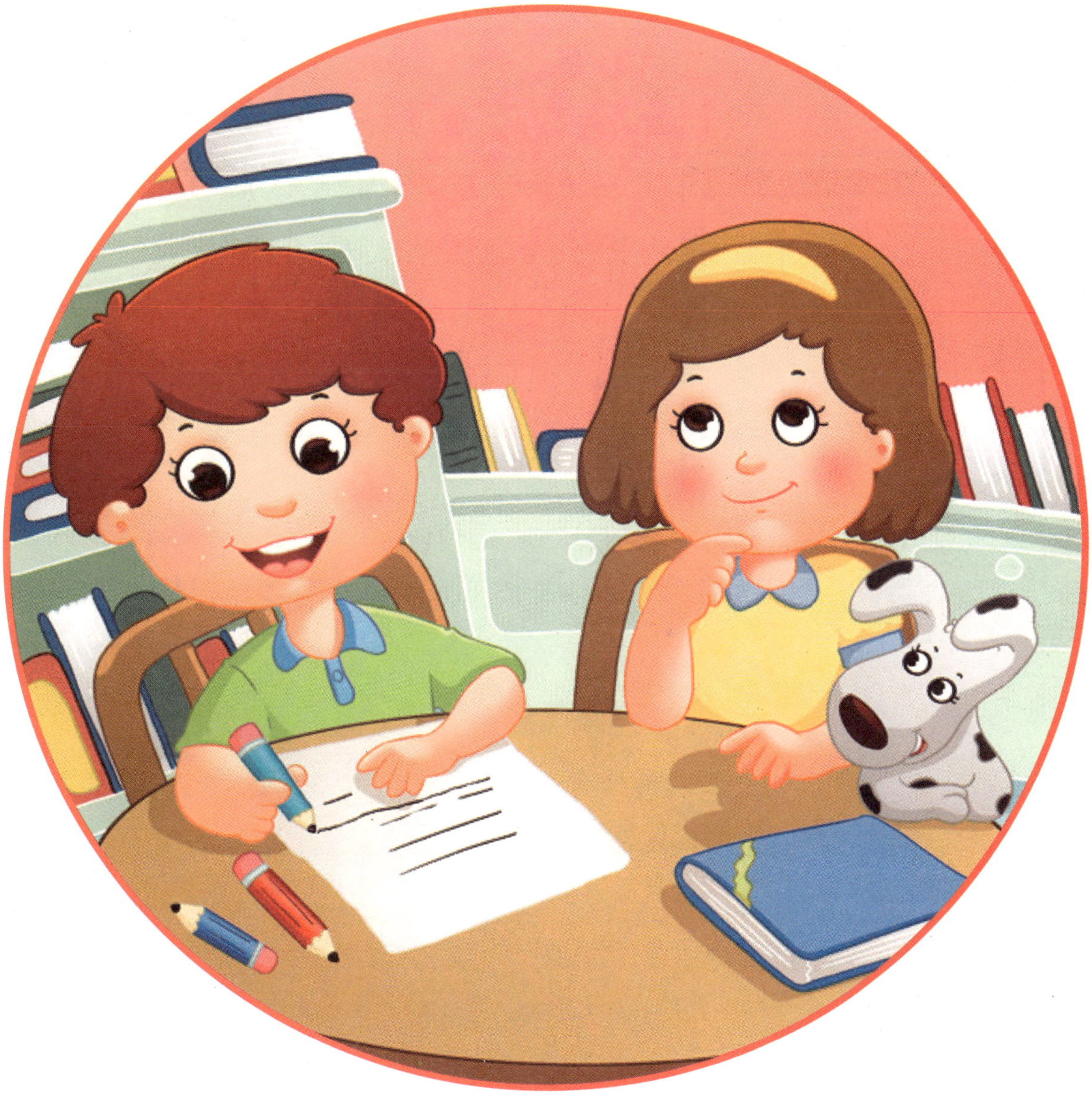

An imprint of Om Books International

Writing a Title

A title is a word or group of words that describe what a picture, text or story is about.

Titles:

- are interesting
- are short
- tell what the picture is about

Choose a Title

What is each picture about? Circle the best title.

1. Hot sun
   My New Umbrella
   A Sunny Day

2. Big and Small Cars
   Going to School
   Too Much Traffic

3. Run and Run
   Running a Race
   Big Shoes

Write a Title

Write a title to tell what each picture is about.

1. ______________________________

2. ______________________________

3. ______________________________

What is Happening?

What is happening in these pictures? Write some sentences of your own to describe these pictures.

QUICK CHECK

Make sure each sentence begins with a capital letter and ends with a period.

Using Describing Words in Writing

A detail is a small piece of information that helps readers know about what we write. We use describing words to add detail to our text. Describing words tell us how something looks, feels, sounds, smells or tastes.

Yesterday, Neo went to see penguins. He wrote:

Penguins have legs.

Neo did not use describing words to write about the penguin's legs. We can add a word to help the reader know about the penguin's legs.

short
Penguins have ^ legs.

Read Neo's sentences about penguins. Add describing words to the sentences where you find this symbol (^).

1. The penguin is a ^ bird.

2. It has a ^ body.

3. It has ^ feathers than most birds.

4. Penguins are ^ swimming birds.

5. They are ^ birds and are found in groups.

Use Describing Words in Writing

Look at the pictures. Write some sentences about them using describing words. The first one for each picture has been done for you.

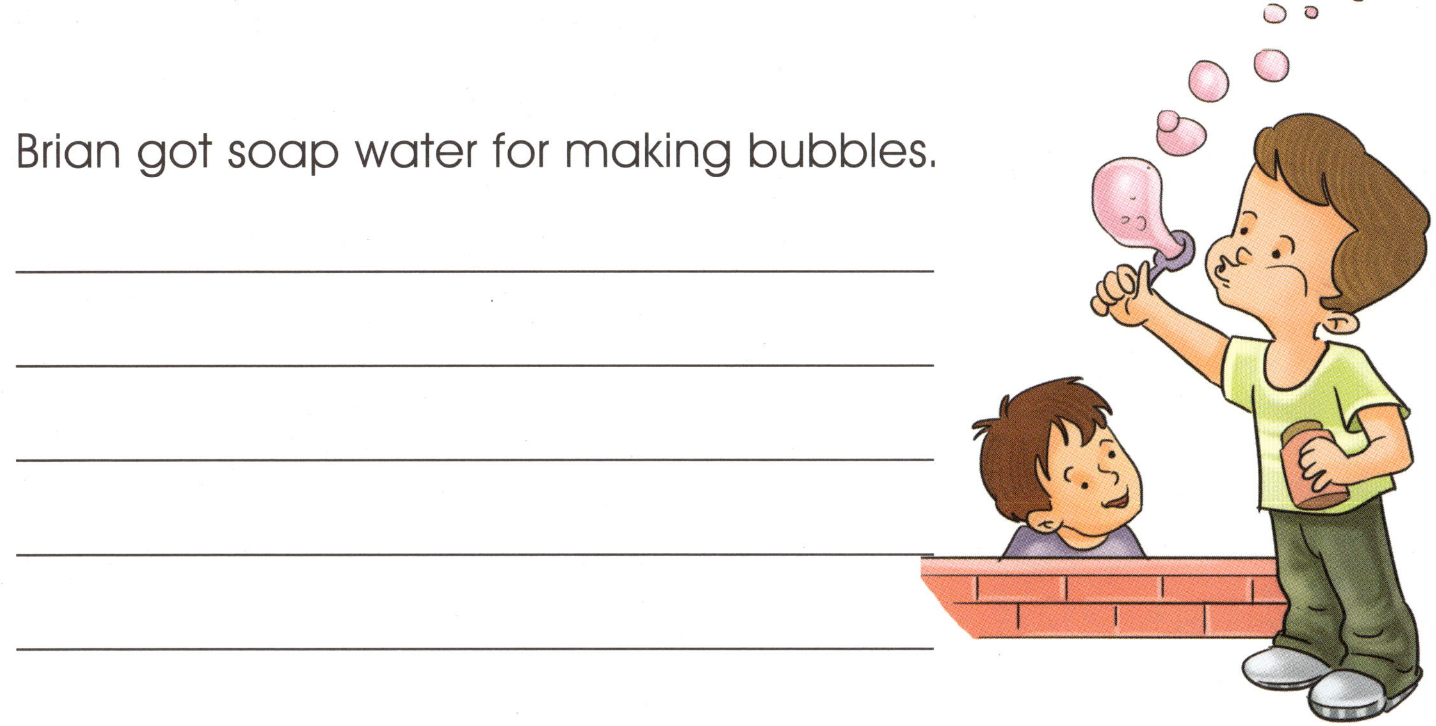

Brian got soap water for making bubbles.

Mother bought a new bike for Kelly.

Write a detail

Now write some sentences about your visit to the market last time. Answer each question. Include at least one describing word in each sentence.

1. What did you see in the market? Was it big, small or many?

___

2. What did you hear? Were the sounds loud or soft?

___

3. What did you buy? Was it bumpy, hard, soft?

___

4. Did you have something to eat? How did it taste?

___

5. How did you feel to go to the market? Tired, fun or happy?

___

Things To Do!

We do many things every day. There are some things that we do every day. On other days, we do different things. It is fun to write about what we do.

What do you do every day? Make a list of tasks and write them below.

1. ______________________________

2. 

3. 

4. 

5. ______________________________

6. ______________________________

7. ______________________________

8. ______________________________

9. ______________________________

10. ______________________________

Things To DO

Write some sentences about what you have done today.

Remember to put the events in order.

Write about Sunday.

Now, write some sentences about what you do on a Sunday.

I Feel...

How do you feel today? Pick words from the word bank. Draw a picture that shows how you feel.

Now write 2–3 sentences about how you feel. Add details about why you feel this way.

____

____

____

____

____

How Do You Feel?

Imagine it is your birthday and you have a party planned. How do you feel? Draw a picture. Then write 5 sentences telling how you feel.

Pretend that you participated in a race or game. You tried hard but did not win. How would you feel? Draw a picture and write a few sentences about it.

Writing About Places

Daniel wrote a few sentences about his room. Read them.

1. The room is big and has walls.
2. There is some furniture in the room.
3. There is a cupboard to keep things.
4. There are lots of things on the shelf.
5. I decorate my room with balloons on my birthday.

He did not write details about some things.

For example: In the first sentence, Daniel has written about the size of the room but what do "many things" look like? We cannot understand because we do not know what these things are.

Let's write a new sentence to describe Daniel's room.

1. The room is big and has green walls.

Now we know what is on the wall.

Use words to describe just what you want the readers to know about Daniel's room.

1. ______________________________

2. ______________________________

3. ______________________________

4. ______________________________

5. ______________________________

Now write about your room. Add as many details as you can.

____

____

____

____

____

____

____

____

____

____

Writing About a Place You Visited

You must have visited a park, a restaurant and a market. Write a few sentences about any one place. Use details to help the readers know about the place.

Quick Check

Look back at your sentences. Do they start with a capital letter and end with a period? Do they have all necessary details about the place you have written.

I Can Imagine

What if you could create a new park? Would your park have different swings? Would it have fountains, picnic tables, barbeque grills? Close your eyes and imagine your new park. Write some words that tell what you "see" in this park.

Imagine your park again. What colours do you see? What do you hear and smell? What do different things feel like? Write some sentences that tell what things in your park look, feel, sound and smell like.

Write What You Think

Imagine it is a rainy Sunday. What will you do? Use the word bank to write sentences of your own.

When Did it Happen?

Look at the pictures below. Write **first, next** and **last**. These are called **time-order words**.

When Did it Happen?

Now write sentences to show the order of events. Write one sentence about each picture.

First, ____.

Next, ____.

Last, ____.

First, ____.

Next, ____.

Last, ____.

When Did it Happen?

In a story, we usually tell what happens in order. First, one thing happens. Then, another thing happens, and so on.

Write what is happening in these pictures. Then, add more sentences and write what happened next and at last for these pictures.

What is a Story?

A story tells about people, places or animals. A good story is interesting for the reader to read. It also has **describing words** that tell us about the characters, where the story takes place and what happens.

A story has:

- some characters
- a beginning, a middle and an end

Read the story carefully. Think about what happens at the beginning and in the middle.

Polly Makes a Snake

Mac and Polly are camping in the yard. They have their flashlights and some tasty snacks. Mac swings his flashlight around in the big tent. Hoot! Hoot! He makes scary noises. Polly is not scared. She remembers what she learnt in school about shadows. A solid object in front of light makes a shadow.

She shines her flashlight on the side of the tent. She puts her hand in front of the light. She twists her hand around. "Look, a snake!" Polly says. Mac jumps. Then he sees that it is only a shadow. They laugh and laugh together.

Read the story again. Can you find the ending of the story? Underline it.

Answer these questions about the story Polly Makes a Snake.
Look back on page 22 if you need.

1. Who are the characters in the story?

_______________________ _______________________

2. What happens at the beginning, in the middle and at the end of the story?

Beginning

Middle

End

3. Which words are used to describe the tent, snacks and noises? Can you use some other describing words for these words?

____

____

____

Writing the Title of a Story

The title of a story tells us what the story is about.

Ollie is an owl. It has big eyes. Ollie's wings have soft feathers. Ollie can see well in the dark and likes to hunt at night. "I can turn my head almost all the way around." Ollie says. That helps Ollie find animals. Ollie has sharp claws too. They help it catch small animals. Ollie has a strong beak. The beak helps it carry its food.

1. What is the best title for the story? Circle your choice.

A. Ollie's Day B. Ollie, the owl C. Ollie hunts at night

Paula visits Farmer Jack's pumpkin farm. It is a huge field of pumpkins. The pumpkins grow on vines. Farmer Jack shows her a perfect pumpkin.

"This is the stem," he says. "It is attached to the vine."

The outside of the pumpkin is the rind and the lines are called ribs. He cuts the pumpkin in half. Paula touches the seeds and pulp inside. It is sticky and gooey! Farmer Jack gives her roasted pumpkin seeds. They are crunchy!

2. What is the best title for the story? Circle your choice.

A. Mixed up day B. Perfect Pumpkin

C. Paula at the Pumpkin Farm

Writing Title of a Story

Read the stories given below. Choose the best title for each story from the help box and write it on the line.

Dog and Ball, My pet Jilly, A Helicopter Ride, Flying Helicopter

____

I have a dog. Her name is Jilly. She loves to play catch. She uses her teeth to pick the ball I throw. Then she runs to me and gives me the ball. She raises her ears when she hears a voice. Jilly barks if she sees a stranger. She barks loudly to protect me.

____

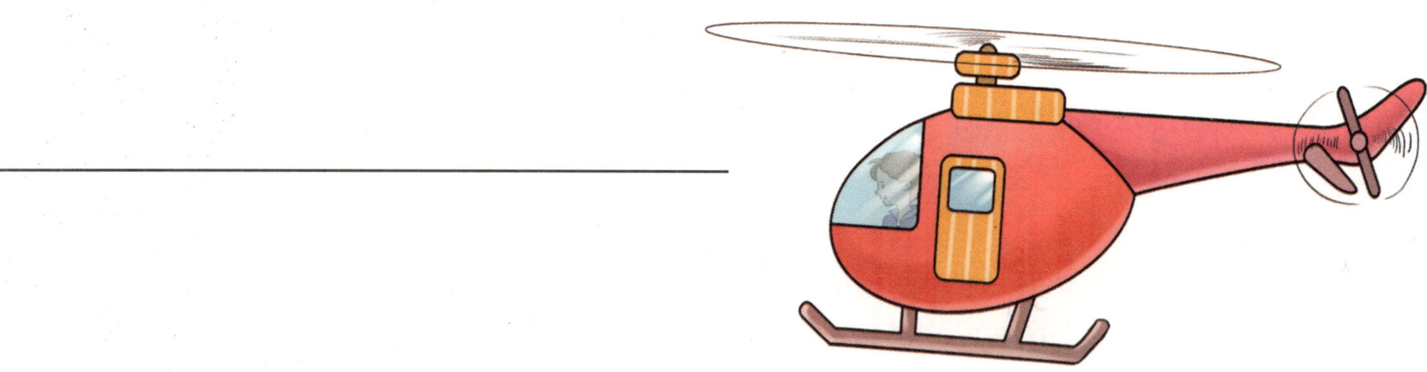

Kim and his mother went to an airport. "Those helicopters are huge!" Kim said. "Helicopters can land in small places," said his mother. "They can also fly side to side." A man came over. "I can take you for a ride in one," he said.
Sam and his mother buckled up. The blades of the helicopter spun around. Whirr! Whirr! Up went the helicopter. Kim looked down at his town. It was a great ride!

Writing a Story

Look at the picture. Think of a story you might write about the people or the place in the picture.

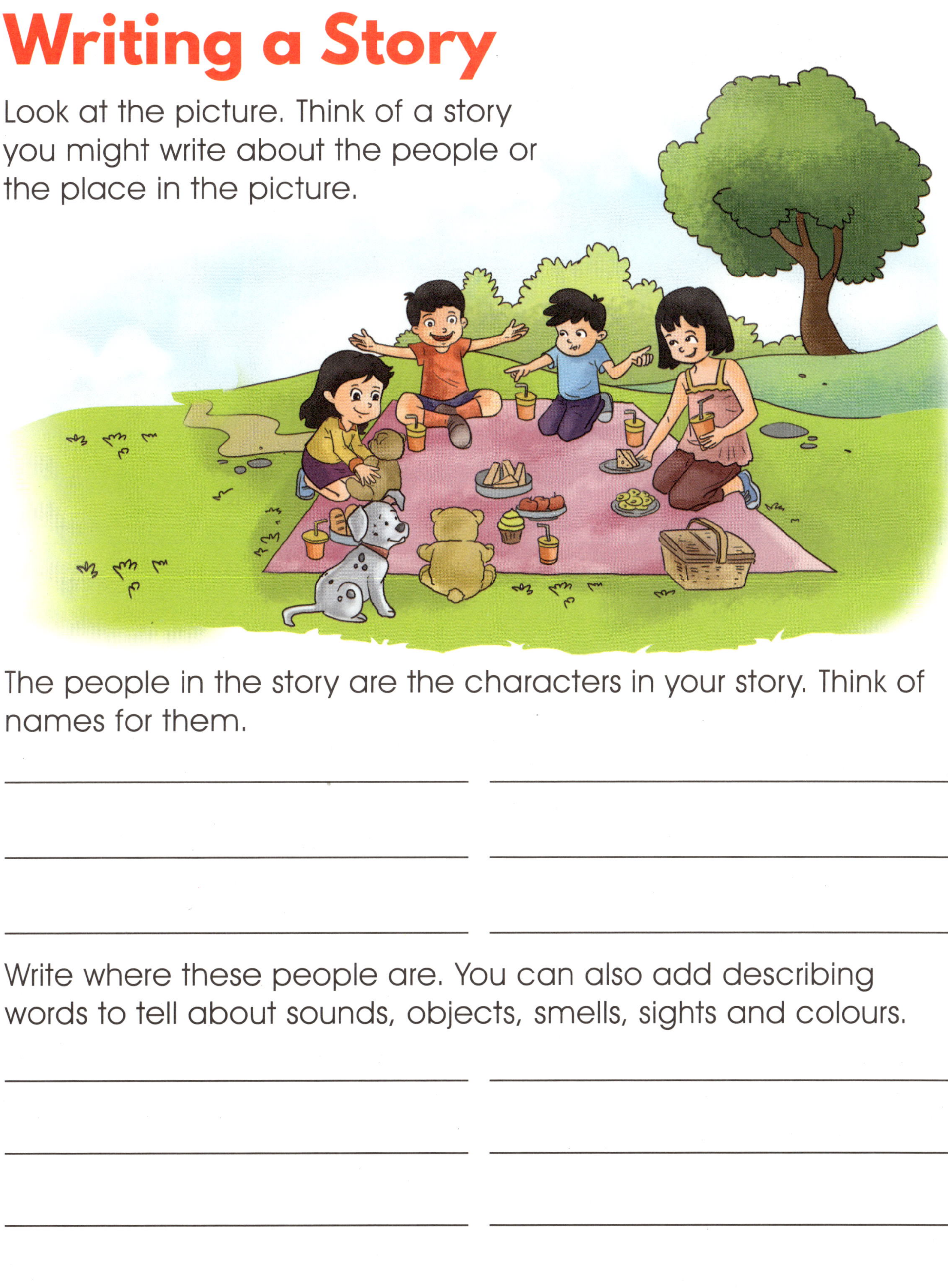

The people in the story are the characters in your story. Think of names for them.

______________________ ______________________

______________________ ______________________

______________________ ______________________

Write where these people are. You can also add describing words to tell about sounds, objects, smells, sights and colours.

______________________ ______________________

______________________ ______________________

______________________ ______________________

______________________ ______________________

Look at the picture on page 25 again. Write interesting things that you think will happen in the beginning, in the middle and at the end of your story.

Beginning

Middle

End

Now write your complete story here. Think of all the ideas you wrote on pages 25 and 26. Give your story a title. Use lots of describing words to make your story interesting.

It's Fun to Tell

It is fun to tell about things that we see or that happen– an interesting bird, a football game, your birthday party, a visit to the zoo or your garden.

Make notes about a visit to the zoo. Write about interesting things you saw there. First write down a few things to keep your ideas in order. Then write about what you saw in detail.

Notes

Went to the zoo

Many wild animals

Tiger then panda

Big ostrich eggs

No teasing

The Writing Process: Telling About People

My Best Friend

Write ten sentences to tell your parents about your best friend. Add a lot of information about him/her. You can take the help of the hint box.

- How old is he?
- Where does he live?
- What are his hobbies?
- Is he kind?
- How helpful is he?
- Which games does he like to play?
- Why do you like him?
- Do you quarrel?
- How do you spend time with him?

The Writing Process: Facts and Opinions

A **fact** tells us something that is true and can be proven.
An **opinion** tells us how a person feels about something. It might tell that you like or dislike something.

For example:

A lion is a wild animal. (Fact)
Lion is the most wonderful animal. (Opinion)

Pick any two topics from the box alongside and write some facts about them.

Tiger
The game football
Summer Season
Ice creams
A pond
Zoo

____

____

____

____

____

____

Now write 3–4 sentences that show your opinion on the topic you wrote above.

____

____

____

____

____

____

My Favourite Story

Think of stories you have read. Write their titles on the lines below.

Stories on animals	Stories on prince and princesses
______________________	______________________
______________________	______________________

Magical Stories	Adventure Stories
______________________	______________________
______________________	______________________

Look at the story titles. Which one do you like the best? Draw a star beside its title. Now write about the story in short and why you find it the best.

____

____

____

____

____

____

____

____

____

Answer Key

Page 3

1. A Sunny Day
2. Too Much Traffic
3. Running a Race

Page 18

next	last	first

last	first	next

Page 22

Mac, Polly

Children will write the beginning, middle and end on their own.

Words used to describe tent, snacks and noises are:

Tent: big

Snacks: tasty

Noises: scary

Page 23:

1. Ollie, the owl
2. Paula at the Pumpkin Farm

Page 24

1. My pet Jilly
2. A helicopter ride